# Resin Charm and Pe

## Monica Peralta

Resin Charm and Pendant Tutorial

Copyright © 2014 by Monica Peralta

Edited by Megan Floto

# Table of Contents

## About this guide

This guide was created to help those who have an interest in learning how to make resin art pendants, designed to be a very easy, plain-and-simple tutorial to get you started on your way. Whether your goal is a homegrown business or a new outlet for creativity, this guide will show you how to create beautiful, high-gloss resin art / photo pendants and charms. In this manual, I break down the process of preparing and creating resin pendants into user-friendly steps that anyone can follow. My intention is to help the artists among us who need some ideas on where to begin and to encourage those who think that working with resin in messy, frustrating, or daunting.

I began making resin pendants over ten years ago and have been fortunate enough to be able to sell my jewelry at craft fairs, in stores, and online. I first became interested in creating photo pendants for myself and relatives and, after investigation, found that resin is the perfect media to capture photos, art, and other ephemera forever. With trail, lots of error, and even more experimentation, I have adapted a process that has worked for me and many other crafters and artists.

Resin work is very rewarding, and there is nothing like seeing the finished product or the joy that the keepsake brings to the special person who will cherish it. I hope that you find this guide valuable in your own crafting.

Please be sure to read this whole guide and the resin manufacturer's directions before attempting to use resin in your home or studio.

***Good luck and have fun!***

# Materials Needed

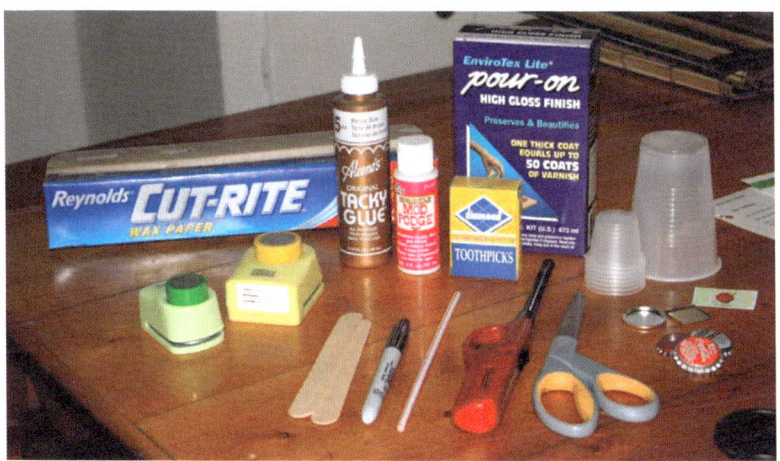

- 8 oz or smaller hard plastic cups

(make sure it has a flat bottom)

- Wooden Popsicle sticks

- Toothpicks

- Wax paper

- Drinking straws

- Bezels & bottle caps

- Art, photos, word clippings that fit inside your bezels

- Latex gloves

- Large jump rings

- Craft glue

- Permanent marker

- Glitter

- Acetone or nail polish remover

- Resin

**Tip:** I love filling old lockets with special photos and resin. I find these at antique stores, garage sales, swap meets, etc. These lockets make great keepsakes and gifts!

# Tools Needed

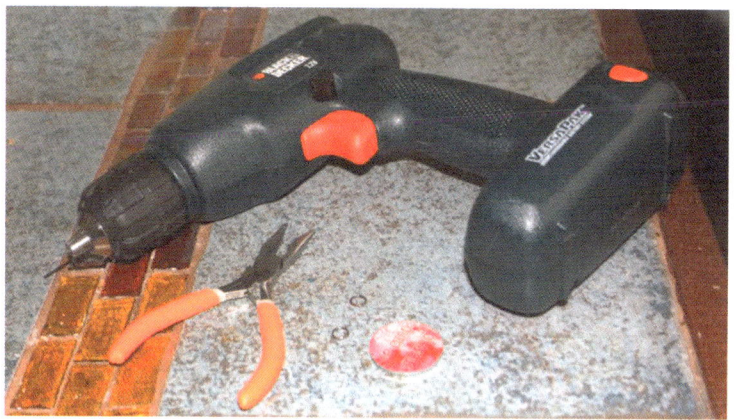

- Scissors

- Pliers

- Electric Drill

- Diamond tip drill bits

- BBQ / Wand / Torch lighter

- Chemical grade dust mask

## Ideal Work Space

- Dust –free, clutter- free
- Good lighting
- Well ventilated
- Low traffic (pets, people, etc)

Bezels vs. Molds

In addition to filling bezels with photos and resin, you can also use resin jewelry molds to create pendants and charms.

I have also used plastic painter's paint wells, available from any craft store. These are great when using dried flowers, collages, and miniature items such as watch parts, keys, beads, etc. Covering game tiles – Scrabble®, mahjong, dominoes – also works well.

# About Resin

Resin is available at nearly every craft store and is very affordable. I usually purchase an 8 oz. kit because I live in a very hot, dry environment and resin has a tendency to discolor (yellow) in the heat. For the purposes of this tutorial, we will be working with just a small amount (less than 1.5 oz) of resin.

Most professional–grade resin cures to a thick, glossy coating in about 8 hours at 70°F, and reaches full strength and toughness in about 48 hours. If you are looking for a glossy shine on your pendants, Envirotex Lite Pour On™ resin is the best to work with; it has a nice high-gloss finish with more of an "under-glass" look and feel.

Either way, the instructions are same for whichever you decide to use. Most resins are two-part solutions (resin and hardener). These two solutions must be combined in equal parts to create a usable resin.

Resin takes a lot of patience to work with; it can be incredibly rewarding and frustrating at the same time. I suggest starting on projects that are less than ½" thick. As with anything, practice makes perfect.

# Part I – Bezel and Image Preparation

Decide what images, newspaper clippings, scanned photos, or artwork will fit into the bezels and bottle caps you have chosen to use. Empty bezels and pendants are becoming more widely available at craft stores and there are a number of places online that have a great selection.

I use scissors to cut just about all of my images. I have tried a number of different paper cutters, but they rarely match the exact size I need for the bezel I am using. Begin placing your images inside of the empty bezel spaces. Most of the time, the fit will be snug enough so that no glue is needed to hold the image in place. If you find that your image is too loose inside the bezel, I recommend using a very small amount of craft glue. I have also had luck using glitter-glue or sparkle-paste for projects where I was going for a glittery effect. In either case, once you use glue inside the bezel, you need to make sure it has completely dried before continuing. I usually will leave any glued pieces to dry overnight before I pour resin into the bezel.

Un-pressed bottle caps are easy to use and great to practice on! Bezels of all shapes and sizes can be used for charms and pendants.

## Part II – Resin Work

Take a large piece of wax paper 1 to 2 feet long and cover your table top or workspace. I have used all types of table covers and wax paper is by far the best since nothing permanently sticks to it and it is disposable.

● Gather all of your prepared bezels; make sure they are completely dried (if you used glue on the images).

Make sure there is not any dust, hair, or small paper particle(s) that may have fallen into the bezel while you were working.

● Line up your bezels, giving them about 1 to 2 inches of space between each one.

● Now, put on your gloves and dust mask.

*Consider the amount of resin you will need for your project. I have found that I can create up to 8 pendants (1 ¼" wide X ¼" deep) with only 1 oz of resin. These pendants are roughly the size of a bottle cap. Also consider how deep each bezel is when determining how much resin to use.*

- A good rule of thumb is to make small batches and complete them using the same resin.

- You should never mix different batches of resin in the same bezel because it will not cure properly.

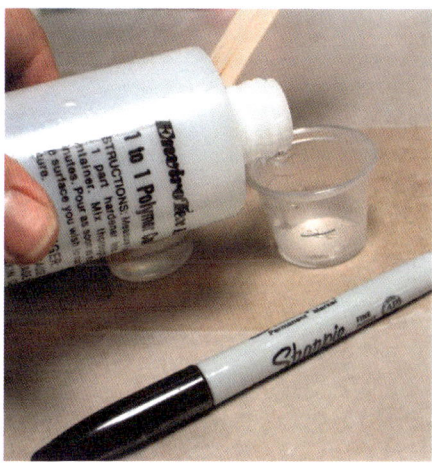

## Mixing

For the purposes of this tutorial we will work with 1 oz of resin.

Take equal parts of resin and hardener (½ oz of each) and add them into the plastic cup. Take your wooden Popsicle stick and begin stirring the liquid well. Make sure to scrape the sides and bottom of the cup while you stir. Mixing / stirring are very important and will take a few minutes to create the desired results. The mixing containers must have smooth, flat walls and a flat bottom. The stir stick must have a straight edge (like a paint paddle) to allow you to scrape the sides and bottom of the mixing container thoroughly while mixing.

What you are looking for after 2 minutes of stirring the resin is a nicely even, fluid consistency. Ideally there should not be very many bubbles, but the more you stir, the more aeration occurs within the mixture and will create layers upon layers of air bubbles.

If your mixture has a lot of bubbles, don't worry, we can do a few things to remove and limit the amount of bubbles in your piece. Read on...

Resin looks cloudy; this could mean it is either not mixed enough or it is too cold.

Resin is ready for pouring when it is clear, has a very fluid consistency, and you can clearly see the grain on the wooden popsicle stick through the resin.

## Pouring

Using the Popsicle stick to control flow, begin slowly pouring some of the resin mixture into the first bezel. Make sure that the image is well covered. Remember that resin is a self-leveling liquid and will even out any areas inside the bezel that are either too shallow or deep.

Repeat with a few more bezels, making sure to fill them slowly, allowing the image to be completely covered. Try to fill each bezel completely before moving on to the next.

*Above* The Marie Antoinette pendant filled with bubbles!

# De-Gassing

De-gassing is simply getting bubbles to pop. Most resin will de-gas by itself to some degree. Depending on your comfort level, you can either use the straw method or the torch-lighter method. Either will give you good results.

After about 5 minutes, the air bubbles created while stirring will rise to the surface. They can be easily and effectively broken by GENTLY exhaling (using the straw) on them until they disappear (avoid inhaling fumes).

A propane torch can be used as an aid in removing bubbles from a freshly coated surface. Hold the torch about 3 inches away and sweep smoothly across the surface until the bubbles are gone. Use low flame. This process may be repeated as often as is necessary while the resin is liquid. Remember that it is carbon dioxide, not heat, which breaks up the bubbles.

Experiment with both and see which method works for you.

The object is to rid your pendant of any trapped air / bubbles. I usually will come back a couple of hours after pouring to see if any more bubbles have developed, and I will recheck during the curing process – this is the only way to ensure bubble-free results!

## Curing

Many variables can affect the curing time. Climate, air-flow, and bezel size are just a few. Many pendants are dry to the touch within 12 hours and are completely hardened within 36 hours. Make sure that you leave your pendants in a space where they will not be disturbed and where there is very low traffic. Sometimes I will let them cure inside of an empty cabinet.

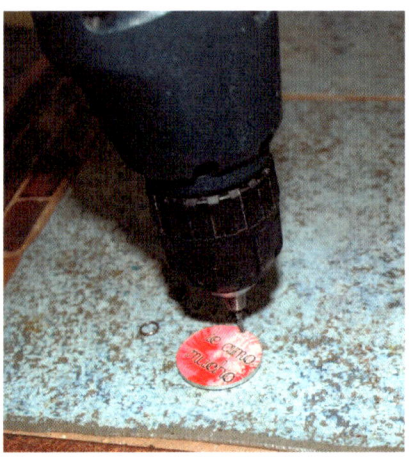

## Part III – Finishing

Once the pendant is hard, you can do anything you would like to it. Drill it, add it to some art work or a scrap book, turn it into a magnet, button...you name it.  Here are the instructions for creating a pendant from your finished piece.

- Take your drill, and firmly place the drill bit on the portion of the pendant you would like to drill into.  Ideally this should be a place from which you will be hanging the pendant.
- Pull the drill trigger and continue to hold the pendant firmly in place until the hole has been created.
- Release the trigger, examine your work. Dust off any resin or dust particles that may be attached to your pendant.
- Take your jump ring, open it up and slip it into the newly formed hole. Close the jump ring... voila!  You have your first resin pendant!

Thank you for taking the time to read and experiment with my guide.

I hope your creativity and inspiration explode with the many possibilities that resin art holds for you!

# More Photos

*Marie Pendant Ideas*

*Bottle Cap Opener Key Rings*

*California Map Pendants*

*Sakura Earrings*

*Keep Calm Adjustable Ring*

*Pistol Annie Charm Necklace*

*Ring*

*New Orleans Charm Necklace*

*Rectangle Pendant*

*French Burlesque Rectangle Pendant*

*Mixed Media Necklace*

## DEDICATION

This book is dedicated to my family, who has always encouraged me to try new venues of expression.  Thank you, Mom and Dad!

Printed in Great Britain
by Amazon